Past Purgatory, a Distant Paradise

Past Purgatory, a Distant Paradise

Dan Williams

LITERARY PRESS
LAMAR UNIVERSITY

ISBN: 978-1-942956-51-8
Library of Congress Control Number: 2017961037

Lamar University Literary Press
Beaumont, Texas

For friends I deeply miss,
Barry, Paul, Ron, and Bob.
And for
Cynthia and Leah,
still my pillars.

Recent Poetry from Lamar University Literary Press

Bobby Aldridge, *An Affair of the Stilled Heart*
Michael Baldwin, *Lone Star Heart, Poems of a Life in Texas*
David Bowles, *Flower, Song, Dance: Aztec and Mayan Poetry*
Jerry Bradley, *Crownfeathers and Effigies*
Jerry Bradley and Ulf Kirchdorfer, editors, *The Great American Wise Ass Poetry Anthology*
Matthew Brennan, *One Life*
Chip Dameron, *Waiting for an Etcher*
William Virgil Davis, *The Bones Poems*
Jeffrey DeLotto, *Voices Writ in Sand*
Chris Ellery, *Elder Tree*
Larry Griffin, *Cedar Plums*
Katherine Hoerth, *Goddess Wears Cowboy Boots*
Gretchen Johnson, *A Trip Through Downer, Minnesota*
Ulf Kirchdorfer, *Chewing Green Leaves*
Laozi, *Daodejing*, tr. By David Breeden, Steven Schroeder, and Wally Swist
Janet McCann, *The Crone at the Casino*
Laurence Musgrove, *Local Bird*
Carol Coffee Reposa, *Underground Musicians*
Jan Seale, *The Parkinson Poems*
Steven Schroeder, *the moon, not the finger, pointing*
Glen Sorestad *Hazards of Eden*
W.K. Stratton, *Ranchero Ford/ Dying in Red Dirt Country*
Wally Swist, *Invocation*
Jonas Zdanys (ed.), *Pushing the Envelope, Epistolary Poems*
Jonas Zdanys, *Red Stones*
Jonas Zdanys, *Three White Horses*

For information on these and other Lamar University Literary Press books go to
www.Lamar.edu/literarypress

Acknowledgments

I am grateful to the editors of these publications for publishing some of the poems in this collection: *Amarillo Bay, Writing Texas, Concho River Review*.

For their invaluable encouragement, assistance, and friendship, I gratefully acknowledge Jim Hoggard, Lynn Hoggard, Sherry Craven, Karla Morton, Alan Birkelbach, Marilyn Robitaille, Moumin Quazi, and the invisible man.

CONTENTS

To the Woman Who Abandoned Her Dog in Oakmont Park

She tried to follow you for several blocks,
running behind as you sped away, the old Asian
couple tried to wave you down, but you burst through stopsigns,
doing sixty in a thirty. She kept
running in the road after you; until, panting, she
slowed. Uncomprehending, she sniffed for a sign.
The UPS man honked her out of the road, and she
paused by Trinity Landing, lost. Slowly, she
wandered back to the park, crossing and recrossing
Bellaire, ignoring traffic, wary of bikers and walkers,
yet looking for a familiar face, shivering despite
the hot sun. Two or three hours later Mrs. Peterson
took her some water, where she waited for your
return. "Definitely not the first," Mrs. P. said later.
Mrs. Urgo called Animal Control, but the Fairchild
kids saved her, luring her in their backyard with
oatmeal cookies while the dog catcher cruised
through. She is a good dog, and healthy the vet says,
 between one and two years old, a mixed lab breed,
short brown hair; she's trained, gentle around children,
playful. The Fairchild's two Scotties don't like her
so all of us are searching for a new home. We posted
signs, "Lost Dog," but we should have posted,

"Wanted: Bitch in White Suburban." When walked, she still wants to head down the middle of Bellaire.

Birds Not of a Feather

Swirling, darting, twittering, a fluid
graybrown mass twisting across Albertson's
parking lot, sparrows in a mad riot,
seeking the stunted trees of concrete islands,
deserted grass cubes in an asphalt sea.
 Then a sudden flash of tropical yellow, and
the brilliant blue of a distant paradise, swirls
and darts among the small screeching
birds, scorning the grit and trash, scolding
the stone-faced boys pushing snakes of
abandoned shopping carts, rebuking plastic
bags of cat food, paper towels, detergent
with bleach, beef and beer, a glimpse of fat
green vines and torrid heat, an unworldly
world of brown rivers, strange fruits, and silent
gods flashing across irregular lines of
sport utility vehicles, all the Tahoes,
Suburbans, Durangos, and Explorers
bound to return to familiar garages.
Such a singular glimpse of exotic
colors and fierce heart, a life liberated
from a cage. No crackers for this bird,
or cute phrases, or comic perches, but
wild flights with unfamiliar friends in

alien landscapes—yet comes a cold climate.
The need to converge and gather compels,
an unspoken law, and the sparrows, knowing
desultory flights, do not mind
the strange flash, the unfamiliar chatter.
Birds not of a feather do flock together.

Mockingbirds Mate for Life

Along the long strip of Bellaire, near the
western edge of campus, where the road
curves around the green intramural fields,
where students compete for t-shirts and trophies,
a mockingbird fluttered on the pavement,
broken-winged, flapping helplessly, having dared
and darted too suddenly and too low,
a mortal object. Helpless too, its mate
circled closely, lunging, flitting, landing
and jumping, urging and urging. Perhaps
the old woman in the white Cadillac, hunched
over her steering wheel, her vehicle
missing a headlight, failed to see the birds,
the frantic, futile gestures, the frenzy
of urgent life and ruffled gray feathers.
In the early morning it's best to think so.

Morning Coffee at Kroger, 7:15 AM, December 2

Old but not elderly, the woman shuffled
three small girls towards the Kroger entrance,
five, three, and two, maybe, all dressed alike
in matching blue coats. The smallest dawdled
by the Christmas trees, wreathes, and plastic elves,
then stumbled as the woman jerked a cart,
"Damn you, hurry up," she barked, an ugly
unforgiving sound. Bleached hair, a watery blond,
an impatient grimace, I offered my fiercest
glare as the smallest sniffled and the middle girl took
her hand, hastening to catch up, the woman and cart
already passing the flowers and balloons. I followed,
saddened by the abruptness, the cruel callousness,
 but still hellbent on a large latte, light foam.

Murder in the Coffee Shop

Smiling Lil wears a blue jean vest, grills
precisely, juggles two not quite covered
breasts, and tortures old men—poor souls
seduced into ordering double toast, extra
butter, bacon, and sausage. Old mouths drip
grease, twist into grins, and cry out for more
coffee—a rare glimpse as she leans and pours.
Lil has several sweet smiles, side orders of
laughter, toasted sticky buns, glazed donuts,
and various cream pies. Leaning over
the counter she collects tips, worn advice,
and the hungry stares of old men poisoned
with too much sugar, caffeine, and desire.
Soon the carbohydrates, calories, and
concupiscence will kill. Her fire red nails
click over the counter and dishes like
Spanish dancers, and she moves well in tight
pants with curious curves—dropping knives
and forks, wiping up smears of grape
jam. Old men with bony fingers poke each
other, spill scrambled eggs, and cough themselves
sick into white paper napkins.

On Leaving Mesa Verde

The Cliff Dwellers left for reasons
of their own—leaving the Cliff Palace, Sun
temple, the work of sure hands, monuments
in stone, buildings to stand time. Leaving
tools of deer, sheep, antelope, pottery
of intricate design, remains of pet turkeys,
gravesites in garbage pits, the old, the sick.

Leaving generations of past,
the pit dwellings, adobe pueblos built
like row houses, castles of stone, and holes
dug deep where gods emerged: found were
a shaman's sacred bag, feather robes, crutches
made for a child, baskets, gourds, spear
points, a skull punctured with a stone
knife—the skull and knife together,

The mummy of a child—the fabric
and implements of their lives. Stories
that died, that haunt. The Anasazi did not
leave writing, tales of pilgrimages, only
the bitter winter winds along the cliffs;
they left for reasons of their own—famine,
drought, war, dreams. Leaving in a hurry,

forever the mesa tops, the long view, palaces
of stone, forever the secrets of the pits.

Poor Apostrophe

The apostrophe took sick,
lingered, then died delusional,
imagining life eternal, a feverish
restless dream, killed by a viral
infection, an ineluctable contagion.
Doctors despaired, prescribed
large lime tablets, sulfuric poultices,
plasters, and liniments to no avail,
finally resorting to steroid injections
and IV drips of precious fluids.
They lectured, consulted, raved,
and ranted while the patient
declined. Mourners gathered,
an aged lot, lamenting the loss,
one or two caressed crosses,
muttering about possession,
resurrection, and canonization,
and some less sanctimonious
intoned, a good life, a full life.

My Other Self

Past purgatory, far below hell, there's an
antipoedean world of otherwise,
a continent of contrary where other
selves denounce conventions and delight in
substandardizations; there my other self
cavorts with legions of fallen angels
disreputable minor gods, and mythic
beasts no longer fashionable, a friend to
griffons, centaurs, gorgons, harpies, and all
furies; he carries an irritable
basilisk named Nicodemos in his coat
pocket, both self and lizard smoke Salems;
unrequited, he pursues a maenad
named Peaches, whose colorful history
has been immortalized on the walls of ten
thousand truck stops; she takes his cigarettes
and money but prefers intimate contact
with a tattooed felon named Big Boy. My self
otherwise spends his endless days writing
wretched lyrics for a rock band named Gestalt,
who ridicule him for clichés, but send
him out to score crack, meth, and strawberry
licorice; my other self is peevish,
boorish, dull, and insecure; he eats too
much fat and grows fat, and he neglects to

bathe, brush his teeth, or change his underwear.
The lesser gods of forgotten faiths and
two-bit actors of old B-movies all
laugh at him, and even Nicodemos
tires of his company and would gladly
abandon him for a better host, but
for the Salems. Yet my other self remains
oblivious, resolute, and stoic;
late afternoons he sits on a rock quietly
drinking cheap rum in warm diet Pepsi,
watching the molten sky, not wondering if,
why, and what for, but where he might that night
find Peaches, and even Nicodemos,
hissing on his knee, finds a measure of peace.

In A New World, Of Glory, God, and Gold

Of Glory, God, and Gold they dreamed, caverns of
of nuggets the size of a man's fist, and veins streaking
across soft rock, a king's wealth a grasp away, and
gentle children of the forest offering reed baskets
heavy with pearls and gemstones, milk and honey.

The conquistadors conceived new lives
that would never be, and wandered along
the white coast and blue sea, hard men
of battles, marches, and hungers, fierce
men undeterred by land half water.

Yet they never imagined what they found,
expecting nothing like saw palmetto,
mangrove swamps, alligators, and reed arrows
tipped with shark teeth and shell. Iron helmets,
breastplates, swords, lances, and heavy muskets
could not contend with the mud, ooze, and
swelter, and natives never quite seen.
Priests carrying silver crucifixes, bearing
the anguished image of the messiah, were
no match for tangled labyrinths of root, vine,
mire, and thorn. Slogging through marsh
and black glade, tormented by waves of black

flies and mosquitos, and roasting in their
own armor, they pursued dry ground and dreams
washed away in tropical storms, discovering
no cities of gold, no fountains of youth.

Brendan The Voyager

Brendan the Voyager, navigator
of distant seas, patron saint of landless
and lost seekers, sailed west from Ireland
in search of paradise, the promised land
of saints and dazzling light. Following
an angel, Brendan and his brethren
sailed in a skin boat, ox hide stitched
and greased with animal fat, and lashed
and nailed to crossbeams of ash, a frail vessel
not meant for deep water. Trusting the wind,
they gave up their rudder and oars, and hoisted
sail towards sunset and darkness, pursuing
visions of saints across maps yet to be drawn.
Zealous monks, they celebrated Easter on the back
of a whale, and fought demons, dragons,
and storms with faith, fasting, and prayer.
They discovered an island of endless summer,
rivers of gold fire, burning rocks, a crystal
cathedral, and fallen angels in a palace,
'til finally, ravenous believers, they
reached their promised land, America.

Antaeus Waiting for Renewal

The old poets were wrong
about Antaeus, Hercules didn't
squeeze him to death in a bear hug.
While traveling to Hesperides,
Hercules stopped to admire
the temple of skulls Antaeus
had built somewhere beyond
Maghreb, and stayed long
enough to have sex with his wife,
and his daughter. When their bellies
swelled, Antaeus took off, crushed
and shamed, and drifted away,
through godforsaken wastes
of barren land, and blistering
desert, until Antaeus, ridiculed
as a half giant, a half breed bastard
of land and sea, reached the Atlas
Mountains, and climbed beyond
the sadness and shame, where he
built a stone hut below the peaks
and fished in cold streams. He's
still there, forsaken and immortal,
waiting for renewal, assaulting
himself with grainy scenes of Hercules

lifting his adversary, a helpless
figure, in death's endless embrace.

Gog and Magog

Gog and Magog have no jobs. Monstrous twins
abandoned behind Wal-Mart, they collect Welfare
and sell a little crystal meth on weekends
 at the bowling alley. No longer interested in
the butchery of innocents, they only pillage
Albertsons for chips, Oreos, salted nuts, and Little
Debbies. They sleep till noon in beds equally fetid,
in a cheap condo filled with filth, Goodwill
furniture, and a wicked sixty-inch plasma TV. They
prefer reality TV shows of hapless fools
and mean-spirited deceivers, but they are fond
of *Jeopardy*, *Wheel of Fortune*, and the original
Star Trek series. They sit for hours in the dark,
their front room lit only by the flickering images of
Alex Trebek, Vanna White, and Captain Kirk.

Yet every afternoon, relentlessly,
they climb the big hill to watch the bloody
eternal spectacle of the giant eagle tear
out and devour Prometheus's liver,
never growing the slightest bit tired
of gore and agony, the butchery
sanctioned by wrathful gods. Gog and Magog
are endlessly fascinated by the monstrous

bird's capacity to shred flesh with its
razor-like talons and beak and pluck out
the blood-blackened organ. Silently they
watch, grimly satisfied with the endless
show of Olympian vengeance for paltry
theft. They like the way Prometheus howls
in pain and yanks his chains, the way the bird
tosses pieces of liver to itself
in the air, snapping at them with its bloody
beak, and the way both Titan and bird seem
to sigh afterwards, both a bit awkward,
embarrassed, and shy. After the bird flaps
its heavy wings, rising slowly in the air,
and after Prometheus turns away to
spend another day waiting on his rock,
Gog and Magog light Salems and trudge slowly
back down to their squalid condo hoping
to catch another episode of *Survivor*.

The End of the World

The world's end is buried in rock
and ice, ageless and desolate, hidden
from time and conception; there
the titans erected a hopeless wall,
half a mile high, and nearly as thick,
constructed of iron, brass, gold,
and fire, to keep back the boundless
hordes of the apocalypse, the horrid,
vile, and misshapen; thoughtless,
silent, and unblinking, they wait
for the gates to be broken apart,
the final uncovering, the end exposing,
for the occasion of world desolation.

The caretaker is an eternal youth,
thirteen, sullen and bored, who plays
endless games on Nintendo and Xbox,
who experiences perpetual delight in
discovering strange pixelated worlds
loaded with dark souls and shadow
lords, where he is stalked by avatars,
zombies, and heartless assassins,
where he derives infinite diversion
in slaying monstrous, alien creatures

from outer space, running down
hapless pedestrians in stolen cars,
and slaughtering fiendish brutes
in mortal combat, he gains unending
amusement punching his virtual
fist through the skulls of doomed
opponents—he likes their pitiful
cries, the colorful splatter, the final
heaving and quietus, and he remains
ambitious to reach the highest levels.

Lilith's Story

Living in the Garden District, with the heat
and humidity, and without air conditioning,
they bickered, constantly, Lilith and Adam,
over the remote, bank statements, who got
to be on top, and all domestic chores.
A high-spirited, too-proud Acadian,
who married too young, who resented
acquiescence, compliance, deference,
Lilith ran off with a demon trumpet player
named Sammy, and refused to return.

They set up in Algiers, renting
a run-down shotgun with a backyard
of thorns, thistles, weeds, snakes, and wild
dogs, but she was content, and produced a
host of little demons until Sammy got
cut up in a fight with a savage brute.

Still alluring, Lilith painted herself blue
and began dancing at the Blind Dragon
Lounge, swaying to the jazzy tunes
of the Luminaries, the Jackals,
the First Light, and the Left Emanation,
seducing bourbon-soaked men who dared

the Quarter's prurience, who desperately
wanted to touch her, into offerings
of crumpled bills, gold and silver, Bloody
Marys, and etouffee at the Commander's Palace.

With her assets she opened an occult shop
on Decatur, selling love potions, amulets,
candles, crystals, incantation bowls, songs
for exorcisms, and the desiccated parts
of sundry small animals; tourists, timidly
paying whatever she asked, assumed her
a witch of vicious appetites and unnatural
lusts, unaware how little she craved or desired.

Yet when Adam's second wife was dying, she
felt a stirring and sent a card sealed with her
florid waxed initials: "I always loved you."

Mappaemundi, or Terra Incognito

How was the world conceived by those
who first conceived, the mapmakers
who first marked in stone or clay, or drew
on silk or parchment? Imagining,
not seeing, they plotted and placed
what they could not survey, strange
lands in distant regions, mythical
monstrous creatures and savage men,
devils and angels in endless
contest, misbegotten giants
and dwarves, fabulous opulent
empires with cities of gold. Believing,
not seeing, they dreamed of wondrous
worlds in exquisite detail and scale,
mappaemundi measuring all
boundaries of land and knowledge.

Carefully the cartographers
placed the Cappadocians east
of Greece, and west of Persia, and
 the distant Vistula became
the eastern edge of dark frozen
forests, and all that was known

was balanced with the unknown,
antipodean worlds of horrible harmony.

Domenico Scandela, Known as Menocchio

They burned him with books, Menocchio,
his second Inquisition, for speaking
his mind, for failing to wear his heretic's
uniform, the emblazoned red cross,
for reading the Bible in vernacular,
the apocryphal gospels, Boccaccio, Mandeville,
and perhaps the Koran, burned him for creating
a cosmos of cheese and worms, burned him
at sixty-seven, the father of eleven children,
on orders of the Pope, for nagging his neighbors,
for spouting impious beliefs, for speaking
his mind, for arguing with priests, for denying
the Holy Virgin Mother was a virgin, or holy,
for believing Christ was a mortal man, like us,
for suffering religious delirium, for resenting
the rich, the oppressors of the poor, for rejecting
the sacraments, for confessing to trees,
for believing the Church was created by men
to control men, for refusing the veneration
of relics, for horrible and execrable excesses,
for imagining putrefaction is creation,
they burned him as an example to others,
for refusing Scripture, for exalting his neighbors
more than God, for being a self-taught miller,

a poor peasant who dared speak his mind,
and finally for playing the guitar at carnivals.

The Original Tea Party

Early historians ignored it, reluctant
to celebrate the wrongs and wrecking, not
until the 1830s, as the last survivors began
to disappear, was it memorialized in print.

A broken business about to bust, unable
to compete with smugglers of cheaper Dutch
tea, the East India Company was granted
a monopoly, Parliament wanting to preserve

eastern investments and tax western colonists,
the Tea Act of 1773. The issue not the tax but
the taxing, and sovereignty, asserting control
over colonies that prospered under decades

of neglect, then the arrogance of North,
the avarice of Hutchinson, all lit the fuse.
Charleston, Philadelphia, and New York
refused the shipments, but Hutchinson's

sons wanted them, as taxes padded their father's
pockets, so 7,000 people packed into The Old
South Church on December 16, and fat Sam
Adams presided: "This meeting can do nothing

further to save the country." People poured
into the streets, the Sons of Liberty donning
disguises, costumes of buckskins and coal dust,
hatchets becoming tomahawks, estimates vary,

100 to 200, divided into three groups to board
the three tea ships docked on Griffin's Wharf,
the dumping took three hours, all 342 chests
cracked open and thrown over, weighing about

45 tons, today worth around $1,700,000, a wild
bash that stoked the fires, the Intolerable Acts,
then Lexington and Concord, April 19, 1775,
the shots and screams heard round the world.

A staple before, tea declined during and after
the conflagration, coffee becoming the hot
beverage, neither Labrador Tea nor Balsamic
Hyperion, dried raspberry leaves, sufficing.
What did they want, these rowdy
yet cautious men, lawless yet not reckless,
who swept the decks afterwards, who paid
for a broken lock, to defy a tax that meant

slavery? Of those known, about a third
were artisans, mechanics, and merchants,

the silversmith was there, as were clerks,
carpenters, masons, and shoemakers,

but the party was the work of young
people, more than two-thirds teenagers,
under twenty, apprentices and common
laborers, out for a night, and not all English,

a mix of Irish, Scotch, French, Portuguese,
and African, all wanting equality as much as
liberty, defying hierarchy as much as tyranny,
to be rid of rank and bias, a free country.

Boston Tea Party Invitation, A Found Poem

Brethren, and Fellow Citizens! You may
depend, that those odious Miscreants
and detestable Tools to Ministry and
governor, the Tea CONSIGNEES, (those
traitors to their Country, Butchers, who
have done, and are doing every Thing
to Murder and destroy all that shall stand
in the Way of their private Interest,) are
determined to come and reside again
in the Town of Boston. I therefore give
you this early Notice, that you may hold
yourselves in Readiness, on the shortest
Notice, to give them such a Reception, as
such vile Ingrates deserve. JOYCE, jun.
*Chairman of the Committee for Tarring
and Feathering.* If any Person should be
so hardy as to Tear this down, they may
expect my severest Resentment. J. jun.

The Pen Is a Virgin, the Printing Press a Whore, A Found Poem

"They shamelessly print, at a negligible price,
material which may, alas, inflame
impressionable youths, while a true writer dies
of hunger. Cure (if you will) the plague which
is doing away with the laws of all decency,
and curb the printers. They persist in their sick vices,
setting Tibullus in type, while a young girl reads Ovid
to learn sinfulness. Through printing, tender boys
and gentle girls, chaste without foul stain, take in
whatever mars purity of mind or body; they
encourage wantonness, and swallow up huge gain for it."

"This is what the printing presses do: they corrupt
susceptible hearts. The silly asses do not see this,
and brutes rejoice in the fraudulent title of teachers,
exalting themselves with a song like this
(be so good as to listen): O good citizen, rejoice:
your city is well stuffed with books. For a small
sum, men turn themselves into doctors in three years.
Let thanks be rendered to the printers!"
                    —Fra Filippo de Strata, *Polemic against Printing*
                    (Venice, 1470s)

Cotton Mather's *Pillars of Salt*, 1699

A History of Some Criminals Executed in this Land,
With some of their Dying SPEECHES, Published for
the WARNING of Such as Live in Destructive Courses
of Ungodliness. Vice is the Enemy that besieges us.

A sinful world is justly plagued with Temporal
and Spiritual Plagues, the terrible Quiver of the Sin-
Revenging Lord is filled with Arrows, direful,
ireful Strokes upon them that Sin Against Him.

But Spiritual Plagues, and such Derelictions,
are now scattered like Brimstone on men's
Habitations. Our Actual Sins are Numberless,
And within us we have an Original Sin,
a hideous and hellish Disposition to every Sin,
the Seeds of all Wickedness, our monstrous
Enormities have been drying this World for
the Fires of the Last Conflagration, and only
Grace can restrain the Rage of Original Sin.

A man would soon Murder his Father and Mother,
Destroy his Wife, Debauch his Neighbors,
Blaspheme God, Fire the Town, and Run a muck
among the people, if God should not restrain him.

Yet upon great provocations God Withholds
from Sinful men the Grace, which He never owed
them, and they break forth, belch out, and vomit
up Affronts to Heaven, Grace no longer Defends
the Soul of the Sinner from the Efficacy of the Devil.

There is a Generation of Sinful men, of late horribly
multiplied, in the English Nation, who deride Revealed
Religion and Blaspheme God, yet there is a Vengeance
of God to Ripen the Nation for an Amazing Storm.

Man is snared in a Bond of Iniquity, he cannot
forebear sinning any more than the poor Animal
running into the mouth of the Rattle Snake, he Fears,
Cries and Shrieks, and he runs into the Jaws
of Death. 'Tis time to look about you.

With profitable Notice, let us Entertain the Warnings
of those exterminated for Capital Sins, those Condemned
to Dy before their time, hear their Horrible Cries
under Loads of Public Shame before they were
turned off. In their Confessions, dire Warnings
from God, Criminals regret refusing Religious
Education, Profaning the Sabbath, and keeping
Evil Company. Yet there is One Sin Lamented

with more Frequent and bitter Ejaculations
by Dying Malefactors, Disobedience unto Parents.

Dying Speeches have singular Use, to correct
and Reform the Crimes, wherein too many do
Live. To Suppress growing Vice, I have Stollen
an Hour or Two and Collected Accounts of Several
Ill Persons Cut off by the Sword of Justice
In this Land, to let the Vicious understand
the Cries of our Miserables when passing
into another World. Behold a History
of Criminals, whom the Terrible Judgments
of God have Thunderstruck into Pillar of Salt.

Salem's Witches and *The Wonders of the Invisible World*

Seeing what could not be seen, Cotton Mather
declared the Devil was Irritated with the People
of God inhabiting his Territories, his vast
and howling wilderness of beasts, savages,
and infernal fiends. Unleashing the Vultures
of Hell, he sent his *Incarnate Legions,* an Army
of Devils, a Terrible Plague of Evil Angels,
to batter and abuse the Good People

with Satanical Devices. In his Hellish Design
of *Bewitching* and *Ruining* the Land, the Devil
gathered a dreadful Knot of Witches for a more
gross *Diabolism* than ever The World saw before,
a Horrible PLOT against the Country, beyond
the Wonders of former Ages, to Extirpate
The Kingdom of God, a Damnable Witchcraft.

Tormented by Invisible Hands, children and servants
shrieked in agony, and houses became *Infected*
and *Infested* with Demons, a thousand preternatural
Things everyday, some have dy'd, some became *Self-
destroyers*, others languish under *Evil hands*, miserably
scratched, stabbed, and bitten, suffering a thousand

grievous Plagues, and sometimes they drag the poor
people out of their chambers, carrying them over Trees
and Hills for divers miles, wicked *Spectres* battering poor
people with bloody *Torments*, cloaking their Torture
with Invisibility, Engines of their Malice. At hellish
Witch-meetings the afflicted are horribly tempted to Sign
the Devils' Laws in a Spectral Book, entering his horrid
Service, partaking of Diabolical Sacraments, vowing

To Destroy the Kingdom of our Lord. Exhibiting himself
ordinarily as a small Back man, the Devil in great
wrath strikes the minds of men with *Poisons*,
and moves about in the likeness of harmless
people, filling the Houses of good Men with terrible
Vexations, goading Witches to sacrifice their children
in infancy, the Imps have sucked them, rendering

them Venomous, till at last the Country became
too hot. But the wise judges allowed Spectral
Evidences, and by the wonderful providence
of God some of the Witch Gang, envious and
 malicious creatures, have been fairly executed.

Behold a Tragick Scene Strangely Changed into a Theater of Mercy

Her death the joyfullest day of her life,
Esther Rogers, twenty-one, a Young
woman guilty of Murdering her Infant
begotten in Whoredom, climbed
the Ladder, leaned her head back
for the rope, and turned to the crowd.

Here I come to Dy a Shameful Death,
and I justly deserve it, I am such a vile
Sinner, Satan made me believe, Young
People take Warning, God gave me up
to the ways of Wickedness, my own
hearts lusts, I fell into that foul Sin
of Uncleanness, that horrible Pit of Carnal
Pollution, I delivered in the Field, dropping
my Child, covered it with Dirt and Snow,

I see the folly and filthiness of Sin,
I loathe myself, I abhor my self, behold
the fatal Tree, O let all take Warning
by me, I beg of all to have a Care, for Gods
Sake mind your Souls, Improve time,
Be Obedient to your Parents And Masters,

Run not out a Nights, O Run not abroad
with Wicked Company, mind the Word
of God, If you go on in Sin, you will provoke
God, for the Lords Sake Remember me,
Now is the great Crisis of Time.

The manner of her Entertaining DEATH
Astonished the Multitude, judged at Four
Or Five Thousand, the Composure of Spirit,
Cheerfulness of Countenance, pleasantness
Of Speech, Complaisantness in Carriage
melted the hearts of all into Tears of Affection.

Young Jonny Edwards

Young Jonathan Edwards hated the dark,
Hated the shadows, the gloom, the murk,
the absence of glint and glitter,
hated the unseen creaking and rasping,
hated the stumbling, falling black.

Jonathan Edwards studied divinity,
Attended the Bible college
by day, studiously poring over
scripture and exegesis, pondering
the predestined plight of careless
sinners in infernal fire;
practicing a pulpit oratory
of dreadful exhortation and portent
to bring illumination to the doomed and damned;

by night he worked the graveyard shift
at Whataburger, preparing endless
chains of Whatameals with triple meat cheese
burgers, jumbo fries, and oversized drinks
for the drunks turned loose at 2 AM, heedless
of ridicule from surly customers,
hot grease, rancid garbage, and rank toilets
clogged and overflowing. He liked the bright

lights and orange glow that seeped into the night,
honey butter chicken biscuits with cream
gravy, deep fried hot apple pies sprinkled
with cinnamon, and the calm before the bars
shut down, before the iniquitous spewed
into the streets; during downtimes he read
over his Bible lessons, liking Job and Jonah
best, and dreamed of ancient Antioch
and Nineveh, of turning reckless fools
away from Lucifer and perdition.

Jonathon Edwards detested darkness,
the absence of light, the dispiriting
confusion of unseeing, the dismal
blackness of oblivion, and the lack
of luminosity. Once as a child,
running in darkness, late for prayers,
he had fallen, tripping over a rock,
smashing knees and hands, cracking
his head, cursing the night. At 5 AM,
after the lost souls, after the cleaning,
rinsing, and disinfecting, he leaves
the orange glow, carefully stepping over
the cracked pavement hidden in shadows.

The Last Words and Dying Speech of Levi Ames, Who Was Executed at Boston, on October 21, 1773, for BURGLARY

Before he was turned off, Levi Ames thanked
his ministers and Otis, his jailer, who cared
for him during confinement, and convinced
him to be mindful of his unhappy situation,
lost condition, and aggravating sins,

Before suffering an ignominious death, he
warned people to keep their doors and
windows shut at night, and travellers
to secure their saddle bags, boots, & c.
when lodging at inns, and he entreated
parents and masters to have an eye over
their children, and care for their immortal
souls, and to all persons, old and young,
who might chance on the words of a poor,
dying man, bound in chains, hovering
over the edge of eternity, to guard against
every sin, and pray God for strength,

But to youth especially he cautioned against
the vices they are most inclined, such as Bad

Women, who have undone many, the unlawful
intercourse leading to almost every sin, and
warned them to guard against that first temptation,
disobedience to parents, and heed their reproofs
to avoid shameful and untimely death,

Balanced at the border of the grave, he offered
testimony to avoid profane cursing and swearing,
a horrid sin, and mentioned gaming, to which young
people are much inclined, which prevails to the ruin
of many, and which leads to drunkenness, another
dreadful vice, then, as a final warning, to keep
the Sabbath, confessing, with a grievous heart,
that he had been employed in wickedness while
others served God, and thus provoked divine
wrath. Yet his final request, words from a poor
dying soul, that no one, old or young, revile his
mother, or brother, on account of his disgraceful
life and ignoble death at the public gallows.

He suffered death for Thieving, a practice
begun early and practiced constantly, a couple
of eggs, a jack-knife, some chalk, unmoved by
his mother's pleas, and prodded by the devil's
temptations, taking silver spoons, broad-cloth,
silk handkerchiefs, a tankard, coats and jackets,

buckles, saddle bags, sugar tongs, a watch, an ax
out of a wood cart, several pairs of stockings,
buttons, small quantities of money and silver
coin, and sundry articles left to dry on lines,
hedges, fences, bushes & c. until, betrayed,
he was taken in Boston, confined, convicted,
and received the awful Sentence of DEATH.

Levi Ames, twenty-one years old, performed
his part on the scaffold, begging God to forgive
his wickedness, and forgiving his betrayer,
expressing repentance, and, fearing the fires
of hell, hope for salvation. Though touching,

and plaintive, his last words and dying speech
were not his own, as his broadside testified—
they were Taken from his own Mouth, a final
theft, committed by printers, as A Solemn
Warning to all, more particularly Young People,
and as a program sold in the carnival of death.

The Dying Speech of Owen Syllavan. Executed on May 10, 1756, for Counterfeiting

Syllavan the Money-Maker
confessed that he was unwilling to die,
his dying speech a warning, not
to obey, but to burn and destroy
all the plates and paper, "Don't die
on a tree as I do." To the executioner,
"Don't pull the rope so tight, it's hard
for a man to die in cold blood." To
the spectators, he smirked, "I cannot
help smiling, tis the nature of the beast."

His dying speech taken from his mouth,
the papers reported he died obstinate,
but he lived obstinate, a runaway
apprentice chased by devils, a soldier
given to take a Cup, a self-taught
forger, he declared counterfeiting "an
easy way of getting money." With four
sets of accomplices in three colonies,
he circulated forty thousand worth,
or more, of notes and coins. Cropped,
branded, and whipped, he cut plates

in jail, and broke jail, and then turned
himself in to save his friends.

The night before his execution,
someone cut down the gallows.

William Fly, A *Cockatrice* Crush'd in the Egg

Died obstinate, did William Fly,
a poor pirate who mutinied
and murdered most ineffectively,
carelessly captured by a captive,

yet he died defiant, refusing
to play the part of the penitent
sinner, or express remorse
for a course of Wickedness.

He went to his death carrying
a *Nosegay*, offering *Compliments*
to spectators, and ambitious to have
it said *that he died a brave fellow*,
he nimbly mounted the Stage,
put on a Smiling Aspect, reproached
the Hangman for not understanding
his Trade, and with his own Hands
rectified matters, to render all things
more Convenient and Effectual,

when called to speak, he only said,
that *he would advise the Masters
Of Vessels to carry it well to their Men*,

lest they rise up, tear down, and seize,
declaring his obstinate Refusal
to Forgive, Fly defied, persisting
in an Unrelenting Frame, damning
the world, his last breath a curse.

Fly and three others had plotted
in a way of Revenge for Bad Usage,
chopped up the Captain and Mate,
dropped them over, then Declared
themselves Gentlemen of Fortune,
and hoisted the *Black Flag*,

but fate had them in irons and sentenced
to die. Despite Cotton Mather's
great pains, Fly, the upstart Captain,
was not disposed, and exhibited
a most Amazing Instance of Impenitency
and Stupidity, a spectacle of Obduration,
subsisting only on a little Drinking,
eating not one morsel, he declined
to appear on the *Lords-day* because,
forsooth, *he would not have the Mob
gaze upon him*, in Sullen and Raging
moods, he broke forth into furious
execrations and Blasphemies too

hideous to mention, he denied murder,
only avowing, *Our Captain and his Mate*
used us Barbarously. We poor men can't
have Justice done us. Nothing is said
to our Commanders, let them ever so
much abuse us, and use us like Dogs.

Drowned in Perdition, Fly was hanged twice,
first at the Gallows, and then in chains,
in Boston harbor, his rotting corpse
picked at as carrion, a grisly warning
to children and *Sea-faring Men* to obey,
and shun the Enticements of the Wicked.

Jamestown

They died, mostly, the first arrivals, unable
to survive, having settled in a swamp,
where the water was brackish, unfit
to drink, where clouds of mosquitoes
attacked mercilessly, hungry for English
blood, a small island in a river bend,
chosen for defense, they worried
more about Spaniards than starvation,
they arrived in April, a cruel time,
too late for planting, the worst drought
in centuries. Still, at first, the sun's
spring warmth, with blue sky, endless
green, and friendly natives fed false,
foolish dreams of wealth, prosperity,
dreams suckled by greed, the Virginia
Company investors, imagining Spanish
success, mounds of gold and gems
scattered loosely around. The first
weeks were spent searching for
the mounds, digging, turning rocks
over, building a stockade, eating
native food, drinking English beer.
They came to reap, not to plant,
most hoping to pluck and depart,

of the first 108 settlers, half were
gentlemen, unaccustomed to hard
work, with them they brought only
a handful to build but none to sow
and seed, only 7 carpenters and
2 bricklayers, sprinkled in were
5 soldiers, 4 boys, a barber, a sailor,
a drummer, a preacher, a fisherman,
and 12 unskilled laborers, who
indentured their lives for a dream.

Mortality rates were catastrophic,
of the 108, only 38 survived the first
winter, and during the Starving Time,
500 were reduced to 60, the living
unable to bury the dead; from 1607
to 1624, 6,000 arrived but only
1,200 survived. They died, mostly,
of malnutrition, but also disease and
despair, hopeless and wretched, some
lay down, never to rise again, with no
sustenance, they no longer fed on dreams.

Mithridates The Great, He Died Old

Mithridates the Great, Prince of Pontus
and Armenia Minor, a tyrant no worse
than most, escaped his mother's plots
after his father was poisoned, taking
the throne imprisoned his mother
and brother, then gave them lavish
funerals and married his younger
sister to preserve their royal blood.

 An ambitious despot, desiring the heart
of Crimea, Scythia and the Bosporan
Kingdom, and chunks of Anatolia,
Galatia, Paphlagonia, and Cappadocia.
He defeated the Romans in Bithynia,
then massacred all Romans found living
in conquered cities, the bloodbath dubbed
the Asiatic Vespers; turning west, he was
welcomed in Greece as a champion
of Hellenism, a convenient pose, and fought
three wars with Rome. His friends tried
to assassinate him, but he hid under
a couch, listening, then tortured and killed
the conspirators, their families, and their
friends, another bloody vespers purging.

Pompey defeated him, finally, the third
Mithridatic War, and to raise another
army, he murdered Machares, his eldest
son, the Viceroy of Cimmerian Bosporus,
but another son rebelled, forcing him
 to flee to the Panticapaeum Citadel,
where he died, half slain, half poisoned.

Dying was not easy. Fearing his father's
Death, he had for years cultivated
an immunity to poisons by dosing
himself with poisons, and created
the Mithridatium, a universal antidote;
When besieged by Romans and rebellious
sons, he poisoned all the wives
and children who had accompanied
him, but their dose could not kill
him, and he begged his bodyguards,
to finish him with their swords.

For protection, Mithridates had slept with
a horse, a bull, and a stag, and learned all
twenty-two languages of the kingdoms
he governed, but Pompey conquered
them all, and killed all the remaining
sisters, wives, mistresses, and children,

except for a sister and five children,
who, prisoners in chains, were marched
into Rome, part of Pompey's triumphant
procession, before being executed.

A Sketch of the Life of Jonathan Plummer No Hermaphrodite (1761-1819)

Reckoned to be almost a natural fool, Jonathan
Plummer declared he was no hermaphrodite,

rather, a persecuted saint, a prophet of doom
and doggerel, he lived in margins, inhabiting
empty edges, rhyming disasters and death,
scripting shipwrecks, hurricanes, wars, fires,
executions, and earthquakes into raspy meter,
always asserting his callings, a poor son of Apollo,
a traveling preacher, a physician, a latter day
saint, a lay Bishop extraordinary, a discarded
suitor, an old bachelor, and a Poet Laureate,

he sold pins, needles, ribbons, fruit, and ballads
from a basket, and roved about, reciting verse
in marketplaces, trundling halibut in
a wheelbarrow, stuffing beds with straw,
a porter, post boy, doorman, and rag collector,

accounted crazy, disdained by his father,
marked as a madman, a lunatic, a halfwit,
yet he believed in the divinity of dreams

and claimed divine communications,
celestial guardians, and God his best friend,

a rejected lover, scorned by women,
even the demented and decrepit, for bad
breath, odd appearance, and bookish speech,
yet he professed light from an unspeakably
noble source, and spoke on delicate subjects,
purveying cures for certain secret disorders,
furnishing Love-letters on short notice,
in prose or verse, mentoring the art of gaining
the object beloved discreetly taught:
loveless, he advised the lovelorn,

finding rapturous consolation in red wine,
memoir writing, eggs boiled in vinegar,
he withdrew, a reclusive itinerant, living
in a one-room house, dwelling in broadsides,
haranguing the ungodly to shun ungodliness,

to prove his manhood, he exposed himself,
and produced a medical certificate
as proof, but no one cared. Less than a year

after declaring he was no hermaphrodite,
Jonathan Plummer starved himself to death.

Warnings to the Unclean Preacht at the Execution of Sarah Smith, August 25, 1698

A much sorer Condemnation, some sins, violations
of nature, contempt of Divine Authority, demonstrations
of prevailing Atheism, so many sad instances, so many
horrid and unnatural sins, Murder and Uncleanness:

but especially the latter. Whoredom defiles the Land,
and a wrathful God punishes defilers as monuments
of shame and ignominy. An awful instance, the person
executed for these Horrid sins displays the hardening
and Stupefying power of this brutish Sin of Uncleanness,

her love to, and frequent practice of it, contracted
a fearful stupidity and sottishness. All take warning,
especially watch out for Uncleanness, the inducements
to this Sin are too common, light garish Attire, impudent
and immodest carriages, filthy communications, idleness,
intemperance, the Rising Generation must take Warning.

Sinners promise themselves pleasure and delight
in Disobedience, they take their fill of love, but God
sends them not to a bed deckt with fine linen perfumed
with myrrh, aloes, and cinnamon, but to a lake burning
with fire and brimstone to burn in their filthy lusts.

Within a few hours you will either be in Heaven or Hell, yet you have long refused and slighted Christ by unbelief, you have fallen into great Land-polluting moral evils, Lying, Stealing, Adultery, and Murder, you closed your eyes and would not see, you have sinned more and more, when your Husband was carried into Captivity, you were wantonly doting on your Lovers, you gave yourself liberty to sin, you cannot plead ignorance, you murdered the fruit of your body.

You have idled, slept away, yea whored away, so many Sabbaths and Lectures, and you shall have no more, labour to die penitent, your Body can't be saved, yet your Soul may be saved, Christ calls you, stay away no longer, come away to Christ, be Saved from the wickedness of your heart, and consider that you may serve Christ in making a confession of your sins to warn others.

Children and Servants run loose in the black and dark night, Young Ones wantonly toy and dally one with another, foolishly sporting on beds, unreproved, this evil is prevailing and growing, sinners are greedy for the pleasures of sin, for Uncleanness, yet the pleasures of sin are dear bought, grief and sorrow won't quench hell fire, nor wash away the stain, Impenitent and Unclean persons will be made Subjects of Hell, and a whole Land cannot be innocent, but polluted, that neglects the Execution of Justice.

Storm, Stress, Friendship, Suicide

Proto-Romantic, Sturm und Drang,
storm and stress, more driven
than stressed, defied decorum,
disregarded rational constraints,
preferred veils, dusk, shade
over luminescence, the luster
of dull, dry reason, the riot of chaos,
turmoil, tumult over polite custom.
Prone to violent actions, irrational
outbursts, its characters craved intense
extremes, pain, torment, terror, ecstasy.

A young Goethe, only twenty-four, too young
to be sedate, was caught up in the flux
and swirl, and in six furious weeks wrote *Die
Leiden des jungen Werthers*, *The Sorrows of
Young Werther*, published anonymously.
Full of fret and angst, Werthers worried
endlessly over Charlotte, winsome yet
engaged, embracing heartache, reveling
in wretchedness, he tortured himself,
in constant company, an unremitting reminder,
never to have what most was desired, lured
to what was most intense, yet most painful.

Borrowing two pistols, he told her he was going
on a journey, and shot himself in the head,
death—a twelve-hour agony, most intense.

Peter was intense, a brother assumed,
and knowing me, an English major, he
gave me his favorite book, a slim volume,
The Sorrows of Young Werther. "You've got
to read this, it's powerful stuff." I read
enough to know I'd read enough, selbstmord,
suicide, not feeling his fascination. A year
later, Peter went on a journey, a shotgun
to the head in a lonely field by a river. All
of us, his friends, groped and fumbled,
the weight of guilt most intense. The week
before, full of himself, smiling, he'd run
to me, "We need to get together." "Sure,"
I said, "That'd be great," and walked away.
Years later, decades, I cannot resist
thinking of Peter's storm and stress.

Later in life, Goethe, having moved to Weimar
and into classicism, renounced his youthful
romanticism, declaring it "every thing that is sick."

No Worse than Worst

What's worst? A word past
Limits, past imaginable and
conceivable, a superlative worse
than worse, past edges, past
boundaries, straining thought,
a word exceeding words,
an adjective signaling hellish
anguish, the most extreme
descriptor designating the lowest
and least, the most and mass,
the dreadful and deplorable,
the harmful and hateful.
There's nothing worse than worst.

Language fails, and thought falters,
but Google offers 110,000,000 results
in 0.76 seconds, attempting to answer
the question, but only offering fatuous
clichés to describe what's indescribable:
really, what's the worst that could
happen, do your worst, at your worst,
fear the worst, and worst of all.

Then there's worst-case scenarios,
when the cable goes out, the school
nurse calls, the house catches
fire, the fight breaks out, whens
and ifs swarm with chance and dread.
Worst insinuates, daring deliberation
to paint landscapes imperceptible,
horizons indistinct, pallid and wan
smears, bleached of facet and content.

Expanded, the question inflates, swells,
and distends endlessly past titillation,
beyond tolerable and bearable. Google
goads, search the worst mother,
the worst date, the worst boss,
the worst vacation, the worst sex,
infinite admissions. Best not to search.

The Worst Lies

Googling "the worst lies" presents
71,100, 000 results in 0.73 seconds,
"the greatest lies" yields 2,210,000
in 0.80 seconds, while "the greatest
liars" tenders only 668,000 results.

HowStuffWorks offers the 10 biggest
Lies in History, which include the Trojan
Horse, the Piltdown Man, Bernie Madoff's
Ponzi scheme, Bill Clinton's sex life, Hans
Van Meegeren's forgeries, the Dreyfus Affair,
Titus Oates, Watergate, and, coming
in at Number 1, WWII Nazi propaganda.

On the *Late Night Show*, Jimmy Fallon
collected examples of the worst lies, like
a mother hiding in a closet to eat candy, and
when her kids found her she told them she
was praying, or another mother spraying
wiper fluid on her windshield while passing
a park and telling her kid they couldn't stop
because it was raining, and a father who
told his kids a toy store was a museum, so
they wouldn't ask him to buy them anything.

Cosmopolitan offers whoppers from readers,
like the woman pulled over for speeding who
told the cop she was being followed—he
let her off and followed her home, or
another who didn't show up at the altar
on her wedding day because, she said,
she had a pimple, and still another who
flew across the country to see her ex, but
he insisted he couldn't meet with her because,
he said, all his clothes were dirty.

The *Jamaica Observer's All Woman* site briefly
lists the lies of lovers, including I'm single, I'm
divorced, I'm a virgin, I'm Christian, I have cancer,
I'm flying to . . . and I have a sick mother at home.

Whisper, the secret sharing app, reveals further
inventions: "I lied to my bf about the number
of people I've slept with because I honestly
can't remember," "I lied to my boyfriend
about how many guys I've been with,
so I appear more innocent. I convinced
myself one-night stands didn't count," "Today
I lied to my boyfriend about being busy
because I just didn't want to be near anyone.
I stayed home watching Netflix and murder

shows," "I lie to my boyfriend when I tell him
I love him. I just don't want to be alone."

MademeNoire circulates further dissimulations:
"I've been single for a long time," "I was just
tested," "Yes, I want something serious," "I've never
cheated on anyone," and "Sorry, my phone died."

With tantalizing details of chicanery, *EgoFor Show*
circulates the limitless lack of reality in reality
TV while uncloaking our unfailing craving
for fraud, divulging grand shams in *Survivor*, *House
Hunters*, *The Apprentice*, *Dance Moms*, *Storage
Wars*, *Duck Dynasty*, *Pawn Stars*, *America's Got
Talent*, *The Kardashians*, and *Pimp My Ride*.

Thousands of sites, populating the political far-flung,
lie about the worst lies and liars, and nearly
as many celebrate cheaters, hucksters, swindlers,
grifters like George C. Parker, who twice sold
the Brooklyn Bridge, promising those duped
infinite toll charges, then offered Grant's Tomb,
the Metropolitan Museum of Art, and the Statue
Of Liberty, and Count (no count) Victor
Lustig, who sold the Eiffel Tower to a scrap

metal dealer, and then repeatedly sold a "money
box" that printed perfect $100 dollar bills.

Memorialized, the worst tricksters have pages
dedicated to their graft, scammers like Catch
Me If You Can Frank Abagnale, Soapy Smith,
The Yellow Kid, Hungry Joe, The Fox Sisters who
communed with ghosts, Death Valley Scotty,
the French Rockefeller, the tsarina and
the dauphin, and Sidney Poitier's son.

Sites like *The Cheat Sheet* submit untruths
unabating from resumes, like bogus degrees,
work histories, awards and accomplishments,
projects completed, portfolios, titles, all
manner of skills, languages, and references,
all dissembled in anxious aspiration.

The world of fakery abounds with rip-offs
honored with their own sites, like The Gold
Accumulator extracting gold from seawater,
alien autopsies and UFOs, the Blue Waffle
Hoax, The Cardiff Giant, perpetual motion
machines, Mencken's Bathtub History, the
boy who came back from heaven, the tree
octopus, and The School of Disumbrationism.

Creation swarms with fraudulence, fake
art, fake aristocrats, fake miracles, fake
monsters, fake sightings, fake popes, fake
photos, fake abductions, fake inventions,
fake IDs, fake sex, and fake relationships.
All that's seen or heard is feigned or forged;
inevitably, deceivers are admired for deceit.

But the worst lies are those never told, those
that drain passion and scar the spirit, those
wordlessly, impassively accepted in fear and
lassitude. Silence bleaches life of all color.

Heaven and Hell

Curious concept, hell is, the worst
imaginable conjured and conceived,
the terrors and torments of perdition,
and eternal mortification, where evil
and corruption reign, where the dead
are roasted for having lived. Multiple
mythologies, creeds, and sects imagine
it, a pit where demons delight in torturing
lost souls, condemned to endless,
relentless pain and shame, the damned.

A place to punish, hell is fiery, harsh,
and cruel, filled with lakes of fire
and brimstone, and boundless rivers
blazing with hellfire, and desolate
frozen wastes of blood and guilt,
immeasurable misery, where heartless
devils inflict everlasting suffering,

where the Prince of Darkness, malignant
and malevolent, rules supreme, a fallen,
angel of many names and schemes, Satan,
Beelzebub, Lucifer, Old Scratch, Asmodius,
Azazel, Belial, whose vengeance terrorizes,

who seeks the wreck of righteousness.
Hell too has many names, Hades, Sheol,
Acheron, Tartarus, Tophat, Gehenna,
Hinnom, The Underworld, The Netherworld,
The Abyss, hellish appellations abound, yet

description soon depletes language, agony
and infinity drain the imagination, exquisite
dolor and imponderable immensity; damnation,
execration, malediction, what humans deserve,
felt more than described, humans discarded
as garbage, unworthy detritus, burning
perpetually, the heart is weighed against
a feather, God damns for sins, and all sin.

In boarding school I told Jose Torres, my
Hallmaster, I did not believe in heaven
or hell, or the Bible, a Cuban refugee who
once confessed he could not confess, who
once loaned me two books, one Dostoevsky's
Demons, the other a book on the popes,
neither read cover to cover, he looked
away, regarding a tiny spot high on a dull
hallway wall. Then smiled: "They're not
there, but here, all around us, just look

and you'll see, heaven is hard to find, but
hell, that's easy, it's everywhere, just look ."

My Parents Dating: The Metropolitan Museum of Art, 1939

Before Breughel's Harvesters, she takes
his arm, and they slip into the scene, a young
couple, nervous, hopeful, while outside havoc

breaks. What did they see, two black birds taking
flight over the ripe fields, the cutting and gathering
for the dark winter, the steeple through the trees,

the hazy landscape, the near and the far? Nearby
weary peasants take cold porridge and bread under
a shadeless tree, while the man with the pitchfork

sleeps, splayed, his codpiece loose and untied. Wordlessly
they step around him, admiring the work of sheaves
and scythes, the three men swinging, the three women

stacking, three others carrying, the fullness of season.
In the distance boats wait in the harbor, and beyond,
perhaps, strange worlds. He lights menthols, and she
smiles, touching a thanks, lightly, neither imagining
the grim reaping of blitzkrieg and holocaust.

Her Final Recognition

My mother winked at me, though refusing
the world: a tiny shriveled old woman,
sick and suffering, non compos mentis,
fingers clawing blankets, eyes shut
tightly, she inhabited a distant domain
where visitors were forbidden,
hearing but not listening, declining
all invitations while offering no regrets,
though the nurse coaxed, my father
conversed, but returning was unthinkable.

Life Cycle, In Thirty Minutes

First, the deserted lot, predawn, and your spot,
the glass gates part, then a gust of cold air,
the cut flowers, the sterile smile, your card,
a privileged member, you pass impassively,

into the interior, the big box, the colossal
efficiency, into the changing room, and your
locker, carefully you undress, pick your gown,
a patternless soft cotton, you flex, tighten,

then go numb, the waiting room, taking
your seat. No greetings, only nods of men
too embarrassed to speak. Across
the small room, the man without a nose

coughs, spits, and wheezes, you do not
look, directly. Larisa and Mary, ever
cheerful, take one, then another, only
once cross, when the man without

a nose went out for a cigarette, gown
flapping, boots scuffing, echoing fuck
it and fuck you. You wait while the man
with a softball under his sacrum talks

about his new Ford 150, intended for
a camper and vacation, he's selling cheap.
You steal a glance at the skeleton man
bound to a wheelchair and oxygen

tank, looking down, he never moves
except to blink, drip, and pant faintly.
Larisa lays you down, the cold metal
surface, you pull at your gown, not

wanting to expose while being
exposed. You are allowed a small
pillow and are told, always, to think
about a beautiful place you want

to go, while the black scorpion
takes aim. There is no pain, no
sensation, only the deep rumble
 and hum. Holding your breath,

motionless, they point the stinger
deep into your flesh, letting its
poison destroy you. Mary leads
you back to the dressing room,

reminding you to leave your gown,
in the dirty laundry. You leave,
hoping those beyond the doors will
mistake you for someone else.

Prostate Cancer Diagnosis

Medieval allegories gloss the walls,
fully colored in black and red, bits
of pink and brown, tiny figures, both
demons and damned, dance a dialectic,
agony and delight, a frenzied hell,
misshapen and monstrous, while organs
are sliced, carved, sectioned, and listed.
The stages of attenuation, the grim progress
from and to, a sigh, counting breaths slowly,
waiting—that is not me, that is not me.
Golf magazines carelessly stacked promise
perfect swings, titanium, and mastery, while
bright smiles foretell the eternal greens.

An Author Writing to TCU Press, A Found Poem

You may have
surmised
that I might have misunderstood
what was said then
and confused it
with what I don't
now know.

Annual Self-Evaluation for an Ex-Editor Who Seduced an Author: A Found Poem

In 2010-2011
I think
my greatest contribution
to the press was
developing and maintaining
excellent relationships
with authors.

My Father's Poems

An old folder, creased, stained, battered,
kept but concealed, saved but lost, years
forgotten, the onionskin's yellowed and crinkled,
corners crumpled and tattered, a slanted
scrawl, left to right, a tiny cursive with fountain
pen streaks and smudges, tiny ridges run
together as letters, a hand not seen in decades,
oddly familiar. Reading's difficult.

Lines scribbled in distance and decades,
a distant war across time, continent , and ocean,
7,600 miles between Manhattan and Okinawa,
countless lives lost, the casual savagery, a war
never spoken but in grim, silent stares when we
played war, green plastic helmets and toy guns,
killing each other across freshly cut suburban
yards, rose bush hedges, and flower gardens.

In ships and jungle he spoke, a cryptographer,
constantly communicating codes, the metallic click
of telegraph keys, connecting orders with those ordered,
one of thousands, successive waves breaking against
hostile shores, close to have seen what should never
be seen, pretty islands splattered and stained

irrevocably, inveterately, fouled with manufactured
horror, a taciturn man, pensive and self-conscious,
a real bastard, having never known his father,
having been stigmatized for faults not his,
he withdrew into dreams, letters, and longings,
a young bride barely caressed, a home, a job,
a peace, a future, all worlds away, visions to blot
out what he could not speak. What did he write?

Untitled

I am a child of this war
Born to it, lived in it,
Lived in the depths of ships
In filth of mind
Castigation of spirit
Where dumb machines held greater sway.
Lived apart on coral isles
Where time stood still
And passed each endless day
In endless thoughts of alien home.

Great pity it seems
To me alone
To save the world
And lose my own.

The Question

Science is wonderful, now great flies
Coated in steel, wing higher than the skies
And falling death our hopes betray.
What brave new world
What great new day
Envisaged now from splattered blood decayed?

Untitled

We are the honored dead
The ones you talk about.

We never knew what we were fighting for
Except to live
And failed
Blindly hoping that the odds
Weren't growing too long.

This much we learned
Death is very democratic.

Kwajalein 1945

The storm subsides and in repose
Mounds of earth
The dead enclose.

The sun sets swiftly far away
Rosy clouds
Reflect the day.

Never asking what was never said,
smug conceits of hubris and youth
I never knew, or wanted to know,
a distant war, a distant father. I knew
he wrote and rhymed, once having
touched the battered folder, a mother's
secret, later, when emptying
a house, I found it, stained, yellowed,
forgotten, a bastard's drivel, scribbled
in haste, I knew much and nothing.

Yet Kwajalein is known, a crust of coral,
an atoll, isle of sand, rock, and reef
circling a shallow lagoon, a few square
miles in a blue sea, dotted with thousands
of jagged coral scraps, once known
for zebra wood, revered for its spiritual
powers, but what he saw was not.
In 1944, invasion, 36,000 shells and bombs
dropped, of the 8782 Japanese soldiers
and Korean slaves, 7,870 were killed,
the dead left buried in broken

bunkers, or mass graves, in repose
the mounds of earth the dead enclose,
reflecting on day bleeding into night,
he scrawled lines that far away florid
clouds mirrored the day, a sad, stern,
silent man, communicating in code I
never knew, I knew he wrote poetry,
but never knew he was a poet.

www.ingramcontent.com/pod-product-compliance
Lightning Source LLC
Chambersburg PA
CBHW041923090426

42741CB00020B/3467